A Tribute to
THE YOUNG AT HEART

Lloyd Alexander

By Jill C. Wheeler

Published by Abdo & Daughters, 4940 Viking Drive, Suite 622, Edina, Minnesota 55435.

Printed in the United States.

Cover and Interior Photo credits: Penguin--Alexander Limont

Edited by Lori Kinstad Pupeza

Library of Congress Cataloging-in-Publication Data

Wheeler, Jill C., 1964-
        Lloyd Alexander / Jill C. Wheeler.
        p.   cm. -- (A tribute to the young at heart)
        Includes index.
        Summary: A biography of the children's writer whose fantasy novel, "The High King," won the prestigious Newbery Award.

        ISBN 1-56239-789-3

        1. Alexander, Lloyd--Juvenile literature. 2. Authors, American--20th century--Biography--Juvenile literature. 3. Children's literature--Authorship--Juvenile literature.[1. Alexander, Lloyd. 2. Authors, American.] I. Title. II. series.
PS3551.L35698Z96   1997
813' .54--dc21
        [B]   97-10223
                                                                     CIP
                                                                      AC

Table of Contents

TURNING A NEW PAGE

Lloyd Alexander had written several books for grownups when he got a strange call from his literary agent. The agent said a publisher wanted to do some biographies for young people. The biographies would be about famous Jews. The publisher planned to work on the books with the Jewish Publication Society.

The society was in Lloyd's hometown of Philadelphia, Pennsylvania. So his agent suggested he talk to them. Lloyd did. He ended up with an assignment. He was to write a biography of August Bondi. Bondi had known John Brown in Kansas before the American Civil War. Brown was a famous abolitionist.

Lloyd read a copy of Bondi's journal. What he learned fascinated him. He also found he needed to do more research. It was the first time in his writing career that he had needed to do that. Before, he wrote about things he already knew.

"I hated the library," he remembered. "It was one of those government institutions that my family had taught me to stay away from." Yet Lloyd forced himself to do the research and write the book. Soon he loved visiting the library.

Border Hawk: August Bondi was Lloyd's first book for young readers. Yet he did not think of himself as a children's author. It surprised him when he won a special award. Judges present the Isaac Seigel Memorial Juvenile Award each year to an outstanding children's book author. *Border Hawk: August Bondi* received the award in 1959.

Lloyd's passion quickly became writing for children. Today, Lloyd has written more than 25 books for young people. He also has published six books for adults. He has translated three other books from French. Between writing projects, he has worked as an advertising copywriter, a magazine editor, a layout artist, and a cartoonist.

Lloyd's work has earned him many awards, including seven Newbery Medals. The Newbery Medal is one of the highest honors in children's literature. Lloyd loves what he does. He feels fantasy stories like he writes have a special place in everyone's heart. "Fantasy in its own way tells us that we're considerably more than we think we are," he said.

"This may be no more than wishful thinking. But a wish is certainly a good way to start. There's no law in the fantasy world or in the real world that says some wishes can't come true. If fantasy is a kind of hopeful dream, it's nevertheless one that we made up ourselves."

Lloyd Alexander.

BLACK SHEEP

Lloyd Alexander was born January 30, 1924, in Philadelphia, Pennsylvania to Alan Audley and Edna Alexander. He was different from the rest of the family right from the start. Lloyd was the only one who liked to read. His father, a stockbroker, was too busy trying to keep the family fed. Lloyd had nothing to do with his older sister. Lloyd's mother kept busy caring for a string of relatives or boarders who lived with them. Most of the time, Lloyd had to entertain himself.

He soon found a way to do that: reading. Lloyd taught himself to read between the ages of three and four. The family had an odd collection of books Lloyd's father had bought to fill their home's bookshelves. Lloyd devoured books of Greek and Celtic mythology. He also loved tales of heroes.

"A Saturday night treat was for me to be taken window shopping along 52nd Street in West Philadelphia," he remembered. "It was a dazzling assortment of pawnshops, candy shops, clothing stores, installment-payment jewelry stores, and shoeshine parlors. My magnet was a stationery store with a few shelves of children's books in the rear."

"One such evening, my eyes fixed on the full-color cover of *King Arthur and His Knights*. There was no hesitation. I seized it. From then on, I sniffed out every hero tale and legend I could find."

Lloyd also grew to love the writings of Charles Dickens. "We never know ahead of time what books will affect us, and in what ways," he said. "Dickens was one of many authors who helped me grow up. For a long time, he was both refuge and encouragement. If he helped me escape from my daily life, he also sent me back somehow better able to face it."

Lloyd went to elementary school at a private school operated by the Quakers. He tested out of the first and second grades and entered the third grade. He was the smallest boy in his class. Many of the other boys teased him and picked on him.

When Lloyd was eight years old, his father lost a lot of money. Lloyd had to attend a cheaper public school. There again, he skipped a grade. He entered the seventh grade when he was only nine years old. Fortunately, he had other classmates who had skipped grades and were his age.

Charles Dickens reading to his daughters.

A PASSION FOR MUSIC, POETRY

While Lloyd loved reading, it was not his only hobby. He also enjoyed music. He had received a xylophone for Christmas when he was seven years old. The instrument introduced him to the world of music. It was a world he cherished.

He began to play the family's big black piano. Yet he needed help. Lloyd's mother found a woman who agreed to teach Lloyd for just a little money. Her name was Miss Porter. Lloyd took lessons from Miss Porter until she retired. Sadly, his love for music diminished when he no longer took piano lessons.

"As time passed, it grew hard to remember when music had been important to me," he said. "Music . . . was a waste of time and I had other concerns. I spent most of my days calculating how . . . I could save enough money . . . to ask a girl for a date. The rest of my efforts went into developing the nerve to ask the girl . . . ."

Like many young people, Lloyd's dreams changed rapidly. When he was 13, he told his family he wanted to be an Episcopalian priest. When he was 15, he said he wanted to be a poet. His family did not want to hear that.

"Poetry, my father warned, was no practical career," he said. "My mother came to my rescue. At her urging, my father agreed I might have a try, on condition that I also find some sort of useful work."

"For my part, I had no idea how to find any sort of work. Or in fact, how to go about being a poet. For more than a year I had been writing long into the night and studying verse forms to the scandalous neglect of my homework. My parents could not afford to send me to college and my grades were too wretched for a scholarship."

Lloyd had no choice but to find a job after graduating from high school. In May 1940, he took a job with a Philadelphia bank as a messenger boy. He ran errands for the bank staff during the day. "I felt like Robin Hood, chained in the Sheriff of Nottingham's dungeon," he recalled. "To my way of thinking, working in the bank was a catastrophe." At night he continued to read and write.

ON TO ADVENTURE

Lloyd didn't want to work in the bank all his life. He wanted to be a writer. He realized he had to learn more if he wanted to succeed as a writer. He saved as much of his $10-per-week wages as he could. In fall 1941, he entered a local college. He tested out of the first year's studies. However, most of the classes disappointed him. They were too simple and he didn't learn much. The only class he truly enjoyed was his French class. He dropped out of college the following fall.

When he was 19, Lloyd decided to join the United States Army. "Adventure, I decided, was the best way to learn writing," he recalled. "The United States had already entered World War II. I joined the army, convinced that here was a chance for real deeds of derring-do." Lloyd wanted to join before the army drafted him. He also wanted to help the United States win the war.

The army quickly turned into another disappointment for Lloyd. "They shipped me not into the thick of some bold fray, but to Texas," he remembered. He bounced among several assignments. For a while he was an artilleryman. His job was to load large shells into guns called howitzers. Yet the shells were heavy and awkward, and

Lloyd often dropped them. Then the army tried to put him with a medical unit, but the sight of blood made him faint. He ended up in the band, playing cymbals and then the harmonium.

Then one day Lloyd learned the army needed people who could speak a foreign language. Lloyd was fluent in French, so he signed up. He began a three-month training period to learn about French culture, European history, and French geography. He also learned military strategies and fighting skills.

After training, Lloyd hoped the Army would send him on an exciting assignment. He thought they might even parachute him into France. Fortunately, that didn't happen. "Adventurous in imagination, a real parachute jump would have scared me out of my wits," he said. "Instead, we sailed to England and in late autumn, we were ordered to Wales to be outfitted for combat. Lloyd fell in love with Wales. He thought it was a land filled with heroes and legends. Lloyd's time in Wales later inspired him to write his first fantasy stories. He spent six weeks in Wales. Then the army transferred him to the Alsace-Lorraine region of Europe. In spring 1945, World War II ended. The army sent Lloyd to Paris, France.

SPRINGTIME IN PARIS

Lloyd worked as a translator and interpreter while in Paris. He also spent a lot of time driving jeeps around and trying to write. He still dreamed of being a writer. He knew that the famous writer Gertrude Stein lived in Paris. One day, he looked her up in the phone book. He called her and asked if he could meet her. She agreed. She had lots of advice for him.

"When I confessed I hoped to be a writer, she nodded and answered, 'Yes, if that's what you really want, then you will be.' But she warned me it would be difficult," he said. "What she gave me was an understanding that art and literature don't magically appear on museum walls and library bookshelves. They're the work of real women and men who lived in the real world."

Lloyd also met a man named Paul Eluard. Eluard was a poet Lloyd had long admired. Likewise, Lloyd called him and asked to get together. When they met, Lloyd brought along several of Eluard's poems Lloyd had translated into

English from French. Eluard liked how Lloyd had translated them. He asked Lloyd to be his translator.

Lloyd translated many of Eluard's poems into English. They were published in the United States in 1951. Lloyd also translated works by French writers Jean-Paul Sartre and Paul Vialar.

Lloyd met yet another important person while in France. Her name was Janine. She had a ten year old daughter named Madeline. The war had been hard on Janine, but Lloyd tried to brighten her days. Four months after they met, they married each other. He also adopted Madeline. The new family settled into a small apartment in Paris.

About that time, Lloyd asked the army to release him from service. The army granted his request, and he began taking classes at the University of Paris. "Once again I was back in school, trying to learn more about literature and more about writing. But though I loved Paris as much as I did Wales, adventuring was no answer. I wanted to be home, feeling if I were to do anything at all I would have to be closer to my own roots. Aside from that, I was homesick."

A RETURN TO WRITING

Lloyd moved his family back to Philadelphia. He began to write in earnest. He wrote a novel, which the publishers turned down. Then he wrote two more novels. The publishers rejected those, too. He continued writing while doing other odd jobs to make money.

"My writing time was limited to evenings and early mornings. Luckily, I had found a job—or jobs . . . . They included . . . a cartoonist, advertising writer, layout artist for a printer, and associate editor for an industrial magazine."

"I had been writing grimly for seven years, . . . ready to admit I was no writer at all and would have been better off had I stayed a bank messenger. Looking back on those days, what seemed catastrophe now struck me as deeply funny. I was able to laugh at it; and at myself. And enjoy it. I wrote a novel about it, as my fourth and last attempt. The novel was published."

And Let the Credit Go was Lloyd's first success. It was a

funny look at his years as a struggling writer. It talked about what he had learned.

"One thing I had learned during those seven years was to write about things I knew and loved," he said. "Our cats delighted me. So did music. I had tried to learn the violin, piano, and guitar. I relished Janine's war with the English language and her bafflement at the peculiar customs of Americans. All this found its way into books and was published. I was writing out of my own life and experience."

Lloyd used this formula to write several more books for grown-ups. They included *My Five Tigers*, *Janine is French*, *Park Avenue Vet,* and *Fifty Years in the Doghouse*. These books show many of the characteristics of Lloyd's writing for children. They include humor, well detailed characters, and a tone of hope.

Between those books, Lloyd took his first stab at writing for children. He wrote two biographies for the Jewish Publication Society. *Border Hawk: August Bondi* and *The Flagship Hope: Aaron Lopez* were both successful. Soon after they were published, Lloyd began writing only for children.

FLIGHTS OF FANTASY

Lloyd's love of cats inspired him to write his first children's novel. *Time Cat: The Remarkable Journeys of Jason and Gareth* is about a magical black cat. The cat can send a young boy back in time to different, exciting periods in history. The book is about their adventures in these long-ago worlds.

Originally, Lloyd wanted the book to include an adventure in Wales. He still recalled how that country had awed and amazed him. "Surely everyone cherishes a secret, private world from the days of childhood," he said. "Mine was Camelot, and Arthur's Round Table . . . . The Welsh research brought it all back to me."

Lloyd ended up writing about a scene in Ireland instead of Wales for *Time Cat*. Yet he vowed the next book would focus on Wales. Actually, his next five books focused on Wales. He called the books the Prydain Chronicles. They were inspired by the tales of King Arthur and various Welsh legends.

Lloyd thought the books would be simple to write. He would retell the Welsh stories he enjoyed so much. He soon discovered that it wouldn't work. "I found I had been kidding myself: I didn't want simply to retell anybody's mythology. What I really wanted to do was invent my own, or at least use my own in some way."

Lloyd thought he could tell all of his stories in three books. He began with one called *The Book of Three*. It is about the mythical Land of Prydain and one of its young residents, Taran. Readers walk side-by-side with Taran and his friends as they face the challenges of growing up.

The second book in the series is *The Black Cauldron*. Here, Taran and his helpers must destroy the cauldron. The evil Arawn, prince of the underworld, uses the cauldron to enslave people's souls after they die. This book inspired the Walt Disney film, "The Black Cauldron." The final three books in the series are *The Castle of Llyr*, *Taran Wanderer,* and *The High King*. Lloyd wrote *The High King* before he wrote *Taran*. However, his editors said they felt something was missing between the books. Lloyd realized he'd made many assumptions about what the characters did between the books. *Taran Wanderer* clears up those assumptions for the reader.

The Black Cauldron was named a Newbery Honor Book. *The High King* received a Newbery Medal and a National Book Award nomination. Not surprisingly, many adults find the Prydain Chronicles series as fun to read as young people.

NEW WORLDS, NEW CHALLENGES

As Lloyd's childhood fascination with King Arthur inspired the Prydain Chronicles series, his love of music inspired another book. *The Marvelous Misadventures of Sebastian* is about a young boy who finds a special fiddle. This fiddle lets him play music like never before. The story tells of Sebastian's efforts to save an orphaned princess from marrying an evil ruler. The *Marvelous Misadventures of Sebastian* received the National Book Award.

Lloyd says the Sebastian story reflects his own story in some ways. "I've tried to play the violin. Even though I've failed, it has meant I've been able to hear music in ways that I never heard before in all my life . . . . I make a direct analogy between that and writing for children."

"For years I wrote for adults. I was perfectly happy with it, having a certain modest success, and that's how I thought I would continue. But what happened to me when I began writing for children was the same thing in literary terms as had happened to me in musical terms in trying to play the violin: I discovered things about writing and the creative process that I never knew were there."

Lloyd's next project was another series of books called The Westmark Trilogy. The first book, *Westmark*, is a tale of high adventure involving a revolution in the imaginary land of Westmark. In this book, Lloyd explores good and evil. He shows that good does not triumph over evil simply because it is good. The Westmark story continues with *The Kestrel* and *The Beggar Queen*.

Shortly after finishing Westmark, Lloyd started another multi-book adventure. These five books tell the story of Vesper Holly, a young Philadelphia girl. The books chronicle Vesper's adventures as she travels around the world with her guardians. Together they face a host of mysteries and strange situations. The first novel in the series is *The Illyrian Adventure*.

Lloyd said *The Illyrian Adventure* was different from anything he'd ever written. "It was intended as entertainment—for its author as much as anyone—with a gloriously fearless heroine, legendary heroes, inscrutable mysteries, and fiendish villains. What surprised me shouldn't have surprised me at all. In what was meant as sheer amusement, below the surface I realized that my own concerns and questions were still there, even though set in different terms."

Two of Lloyd Alexander's many books.

STORIES EVERYWHERE

Friends say Lloyd is a very disciplined writer. He often begins work early in the day and doesn't take much of a break until dinnertime. However, he likes to joke about his habits. "I start work at the crack of dawn, but if things go badly at the typewriter, I may sneak back to bed. Janine claims I'm snoozing. I claim I'm thinking horizontally."

When he's not writing, he stays busy with a variety of interests. "I'll go in the backyard and feed peanuts to the squirrels. Or have philosophical conversations with our four cats. Or play the fiddle; usually Mozart, the composer I love best. Or draw pictures. Or read books."

Lloyd adds that inspirations for stories can come anytime, from anywhere. "I've learned that you needn't go any distance at all for story ideas," he said. "For example, I live near Philadelphia, in Drexel Hill. Well, actually there's no hill in Drexel Hill, unless you count a bump in the road across from the barber shop. There's a street named Riverview—bone dry, not a river in sight."

"But if I want, I can turn that bump into Mount Everest, that invisible river into the raging Mississippi, my cats into tigers, my backyard into Sherwood Forest. The real excitement is creating something that didn't exist before. And writing for young people—that's the best adventure of all."

Lloyd receives many letters from his young fans and enjoys reading them. He answers many letters as well, and allows classes to visit him in his home. He is active in many organizations involved with children's literature. In addition to the many awards he has received for individual books, Lloyd also has been recognized for his full body of work. Twice he won the Drexel Award for outstanding contributions to literature for children. He also won the Lifetime Achievement Award from the Pennsylvania Center for the Book.

WRITING AS LEARNING

Lloyd says his writing has given him an opportunity to learn more about life—even if he's writing fantasy.

"If Wales gave me a glimpse of Prydain, I think Prydain gave me a glimpse of what every writer must do," he said. "To say, each in his own way, what is deepest in his heart. If writers learn more from their books than do readers, perhaps I may have begun to learn."

He added that writing about fantasy allows him to explore the very things in life that are most real. "Using the device of an imaginary world allowed me in some strange way to go to the central issues," he said. "I used the imaginary kingdom . . . to express what I hoped would be some very hard truths. I never saw fairy tales as an escape or a cop out . . . . On the contrary, speaking for myself, it is the way to understand reality."

WRITINGS

Most people know Lloyd Alexander for his fantasy books for young people. Yet any of his titles promises a thrilling and enjoyable read:

Border Hawk: August Bondi, Farrar, Straus, 1959
The Flagship Hope: Aaron Lopez, Farrar, Straus, 1960
Time Cat: The Remarkable Journeys of Jason and Gareth, Holt, 1963
The Book of Three, Holt, 1964
The Black Cauldron, Holt, 1965
Coll and His White Pig, Holt, 1965
The Castle of Llyr, Holt, 1966
Taran Wanderer, Holt, 1967
The Truthful Harp, Holt, 1967
The High King, Holt, 1968
The Marvelous Misadventures of Sebastian, Dutton, 1970
The King's Foundation, Dutton, 1971
The Four Donkeys, Holt, 1972
The Foundling and Other Tales of Prydain, Holt, 1973
The Cat Who Wished to Be a Man, Dutton, 1973
The Wizard in the Tree, Dutton, 1975
The Town Cats and Other Tales, Dutton, 1977

The First Two Lives of Lukas-Kasha, Dutton, 1978

Westmark, Dutton, 1981

The Kestrel, Dutton, 1982

The Beggar Queen, Dutton, 1984

The Illyrian Adventure, Dutton, 1986

The El Dorado Adventure, Dutton, 1987

The Drackenburg Adventure, Dutton, 1988

The Jedera Adventure, Dutton, 1989

The Philadelphis Adventure, Dutton, 1990

GLOSSARY OF TERMS

Abolitionist — A person who wants to end slavery.

Alsace-Lorraine — A region in Europe near France.

Artillery — A branch of the Army that uses very large guns.

Assumptions — Ideas a person thinks are true even though they have no proof.

Biographies — Stories about the lives of real people.

Boarders — People who pay the people they live with for room and board.

Catastrophe — A great disaster or misfortune.

Derring-do — Daring action.

Drafted — When a person has to serve in the military.

Fiddle — A kind of violin.

Fray — A fight.

Harmonium — A keyboard-type instrument.

Howitzers — Large guns.

Installment payment — To pay for something a little at a time.

Institutions — Public organizations.

Literary agent — A person who represents writers to publishers.

Mythology — A collection of legendary stories and beliefs.

Quakers — A religious society.

Refuge — A place that provides protection.

Xylophone — A musical instrument made of wooden bars.

Index